Discovering NORFOLK

Cadbury Lamb

Shire Publications, Tring, Herts.

CONTENTS

INTRODUCTION

By the non-East Anglian, Norfolk is often dismissed as comprising Norwich, 'a fine city', and the Norfolk Broads, all surrounded by miles of flat. But the hump of East Anglia is probably more the traditional cradle of England than any other county.

Through Norfolk have passed, en route to the hinterland, all the invading races that make up the English people—Celts, Romans, Jutes, Angles, Saxons, Danes and Flemings. During the middle ages it was the population centre and industrial hub of the whole country. During the 18th and 19th centuries it became the national centre of agricultural experiment and development. During the 20th century it has been, with Suffolk, a key area for the defence of the realm.

Norfolk has much to attract visitors. Its churches are the crowning achievement of British ecclesiastical architecture. Its wild life is prolific and varied. (The reserves of the north coast have added many new birds to the British list.) Geologically, the continually changing coastline is one of the most interesting in England. Historically, Norfolk is a hunting paradise for antiquarians and traditionalists. And in Norwich, with its historic past, its enlightened government, and its civic pride, the county possesses what must surely be the most perfect city in England.

Discovering Norfolk is based on circular tours that cover all the main places of interest in the county. These routes are devised for the motorist who does not want to spend all day on crowded main roads. Each can be done very comfortably in a day. In addition, there are walking tours of Norwich, Great Yarmouth and King's Lynn.

ROUTE 1

GREAT YARMOUTH — Caister — Potter Heigham — Horning — Wroxham — Ranworth — South Walsham — — Acle — GREAT YARMOUTH (about 38 miles).

This tour is described starting from Great Yarmouth, but it can be joined from Norwich by taking the A1151 to Wroxham and starting there. From **Great Yarmouth** (see page 31) take the A149 through the sandhills to the ancient village of **Caister-on-Sea.** The Romans built a walled harbour town here and Caister was a busy port before it became silted up. The site lies north of the Caister-Acle road and was excavated in 1951 and 1961. **Caister Castle** is about a mile west of the village off the A1064. The ruins are open daily. It was built of brick in the 1430s by Sir John Fastolff, a commander who fought at Harfleur and Agincourt in the wars against France. On his death the Paston family fought the Duke of Norfolk for possession and occupied the castle until 1559. A tower and some walls still stand within a moat. You will notice that some walls have arrow slits, some gun ports. Continue north along the A149 following it through **Ormesby St. Margaret,** a pretty village with a fine church that has a decorated Norman south doorway, through **Ormesby St. Michael,** birthplace of a number of the Pilgrim Fathers, across Ormesby and Rollesby Broad to **Potter Heigham** bridge. This medieval bridge crosses the river Thurne, one of the main rivers that make up the Norfolk Broads, and once over it you are in Broadland proper.

Boats pass up the Thurne to Hickling Broad and Horsey Mere, two of the wilder and more open broads, and during the holiday season you will see the yachts lowering their sails and masts in order to get under this low bridge. Potter Heigham church is reached by taking the right turn in the village and turning right at the T-junction. The church is thatched and has a round tower. In the aisles there are traces of 14th century wall paintings. The font is 15th century and made of brick. Potter Heigham was a famous brick-making centre.

Continue along the B1354 through **Ludham,** an attractive, well cared for village whose church has a fine hammerbeam roof, to **Johnson's Street,** a cluster of houses and an inn. The road to the left leads to the ruins of **St. Benet's Abbey,** a Benedictine house founded in 955 and the only monastery that escaped dissolution by Henry VIII. The Bishop of Norwich is still abbot of St. Benet's-at-Hulme (plate 9). The only remains are a gate house (to which a mill was added in the 18th century).

The B1354 continues over the river Ant to **Horning** (plate 5), a pretty village on the Bure, rapidly being developed to cater for the increasing river traffic. Then continue on to the A1151 and turn left into **Wroxham,** perhaps the best-known Broadland holiday centre. Its busy shopping centre and crowded river banks impart some of the excitement of embarking for a fortnight's cruise. Once over the bridge take the first right turn over the railway to the church. From the churchyard there is a fine view of the Bure winding down from Belaugh church. Wroxham church itself has a splendid Norman south doorway.

Half a mile further down the A1151 turn left to Salhouse and follow the signs to Woodbastwick and Ranworth. This road gives occasional tempting glimpses of several wood-fringed broads, but not until **Ranworth** can the motorist really appreciate the beauty of these waters. By Ranworth Broad there is a small car park and a tea room. The short walk back up the hill to Ranworth church—'the cathedral of the Broads'—offers a fine view over the broad. The church is famous for its splendid painted rood screen, which fortunately survived a recent fire in the chancel.

Continue on to the B1140 at **South Walsham.** Turn left, passing the churches in adjoining churchyards, and follow the road to **Acle,** a spacious village with pleasant houses surrounding the main crossroads. From here the A47 leads straight across the marshes back to Yarmouth.

ROUTE 2

NORWICH — North Walsham — Bacton — Paston — Trunch — Cromer — Felbrigg — Aylsham — Blickling — NORWICH (about 61 miles).

Leave **Norwich** (see page 33) by the A115 through Tombland and follow it for half a mile until the B1150 forks left to **Coltishall,** an attractive village, and on to **North Walsham.** This is a pleasant little town with a picturesque market cross and a big church with a partly collapsed tower. From the market place a passage leads to the Paston Grammar School which Nelson and Sir Rider Haggard attended. Sir William Paston, the founder, reclines on his elbow in the church.

Leave Walsham by the B1150 to **Bacton** and the coast. On this road, from Bacton to Happisburgh, are the ruins of

Broomholm Priory, once famous for its relic of the true Cross which was claimed to have performed miracles. A road by the gatehouse leads to fragments of the Norman priory church, the chapter house and dormitory—all enclosed by a farmyard. Return to Bacton village, very neat and pretty with well-kept cottages, and take the coast road B1159 to **Paston.** This was the home of an important medieval family, whose collected letters about their estates, their housekeeping and their neighbours form an important source of information about life at that time. The thatched church, St. Margaret's, is named after the patron saint of shepherds. It contains many monuments to the Paston family. Near the church stands all that now remains of the Pastons' home—the Great Barn, built in 1581.

The B1159 goes on to Cromer, but two small villages inland deserve a detour because of their magnificent churches. Just beyond Paston church take the left turn to **Knapton,** whose church roof, made of Irish oak in 1504, is one of the finest in England. Try and count the angels; there are well over a hundred of them. The weather-vane on the tower was designed by Cotman, the Norwich artist, supposedly while giving a drawing lesson at Knapton House. From Knapton take the road to **Trunch.** Here the splendid, airy St. Botolph's is Perpendicular throughout with a fine hammerbeam roof decorated with angels. But the church is more famous for its elaborate font canopy—one of the only four in England—and certainly the most richly decorated. Before leaving look at the rood screen with its paintings of the twelve apostles, and at the carved stalls and misericords. From Trunch follow signs to Gimingham, and then on to **Trimingham** on the coast road at Beacon Hill, where the cliffs rise to over 230 feet. On a clear day you can see the spire of Norwich Cathedral from here. To the right a mile or so is **Mundesley,** a pretty seaside village where the poet Cowper used to stay. Left lies Cromer, reached via **Overstrand,** a small resort of fine houses (two by Lutyens) but with a coast erosion problem. Continue on to **Cromer** (see page 30).

Leave Cromer on the A148 to King's Lynn and within two miles turn left on to the B1436 to **Felbrigg.** About half a mile along, by a road junction, is the entrance to Felbrigg Park. The road into the park is open for traffic to the church. On your way you will notice Felbrigg Hall, a well-preserved Jacobean house, now home of R. W. Ketton-Cremer, the historian, who has written a history of this famous house. The brasses of Felbrigg church are renowned, the best and largest being that of Sir Simon Felbrigg and his wife. Return to the park gates, turn right and drive through Felbrigg village and on to Roughton. Here turn right on to the A140 and follow it to **Aylsham,** turning right at the town centre for **Blickling** (B1354). Blickling Hall (plate 14) is a National Trust property and one of the most beautiful Jacobean houses in England, set in a magnificent park. Blickling has associations with Sir John Fastolff, Anne Boleyn and Charles II.

Return to Norwich via Aylsham, the A140 (which is interrupted abruptly by the airfield at Horsham St. Faith), and then the B1149.

ROUTE 3

HOLT — Fakenham — East Barsham — Walsingham — Wells — Holkham — Burnham Thorpe — Binham — Langham — Blakeney — Cley — Weybourne — HOLT (about 43 miles).

This route begins and ends at Holt, but can be joined from Norwich by taking the A1067 to Fakenham. **Holt** was burnt down in 1708, so there are few old buildings in the town. It has a famous grammar school, founded by Sir John Gresham in 1555, but the Tudor-style schoolhouse in the middle of the town is a 19th century building on the original site. The church has a 14th century chancel and tower and a 15th century south porch. It has been much restored.

Leave Holt by the A148 to Fakenham, a fast road through open country. **Fakenham** lies on the river Wensum, which flows on to Norwich, and is a small town of pleasant proportions if not of great interest. The church has a fine Perpendicular tower. Keep on the A148 through Fakenham and branch off towards Wells just outside the town. Follow the B1105 north into the valley of the Stiffkey and to **East Barsham Manor** (plate 17), the epitome of a Tudor mansion —even slept in by Henry VIII.

Continue along the B1105 a mile to **Houghton St. Giles,** turn left in the village and down to the Slipper Chapel. A mile from this chapel is **Little Walsingham,** site of the most famous Christian shrine in medieval England. Thousands visited the shrine each year, among them Henry III, Edward I, Edward II, and Henry VII. Many pilgrims walked barefoot from the Slipper Chapel, including Henry VIII, who ultimately had Walsingham suppressed and the famous statue of Our Lady of Walsingham burnt publicly in London. The Chapel fell into disrepair and not until the end of the last century was it restored. Next stop at Little Walsingham, a village with a profound air of medieval sanctity. The priory was founded in 1061. The Virgin Mary was reputed to have appeared here and when the Moslems overran Nazareth the priory claimed the Walsingham shrine to be the Virgin's new abode. The remains of the priory are scanty, the largest piece being the east wall of the church. Nearby are twin holy wells. Of the Chapel of Our Lady, which was the original shrine, nothing remains. Pilgrims came here from all over Europe and in such numbers that what we call 'the milky way' was called the Walsingham Way. Pilgrimages were revived in the 1930s and still continue. The new shrine, built in Italian style in 1937, is incongruous in an English village. The parish church, self conscious in this Catholic centre, is Perpendicular, with a lovely south porch and one of the finest 15th century fonts in England. Before leaving Walsingham note the Black Lion Hotel, frequented by pilgrims for 700 years, the village pump, and the Friary ruins, a quarter of a mile west of the church.

The B1105 continues to **Wells-next-the-Sea,** a little coast town and sprat fishing port attractively laid out round its green. From the quay a road runs alongside the estuary for a mile to the beach and to pleasure grounds screened by pine trees. The Norfolk coast road, the A149, goes through Wells. For a worthwhile diversion follow it west (coast on your right) for two miles to **Holkham Hall**. This was the estate of 'Coke of Holkham', the 18th century Earl of Leicester who turned his barren, sandy legacy into productive farmland and began agrarian experiments that were to influence the whole of British farming. The park and hall are open to visitors. The hall was built in 1734 by William Kent in the Palladian style. The park contains many wild fowl, a column erected to Coke's memory, and St. Withburgh church, which is full of Coke family monuments.

Nelson admirers may continue on to his birthplace at **Burnham Thorpe.** Fork left off the A149 past Holkham Park and turn left after two miles. Nelson's father was rector at Burnham Thorpe and the church has, among a number of relics, a bust of Nelson and a lectern made from timbers of the *Victory.* A road from Burnham leads back to Wells following the south and east sides of Holkham Park. From Wells take the A149 to **Stiffkey,** a cockling village, and turn right down narrow roads following signs to **Binham.** In 1091 a Benedictine priory was founded at Binham. It must have been a splendid building and fortunately much of it remains. The nave of the priory church is now the parish church and the rest of the ruins are well cared for by the Department of the Environment. The B1388 leads from Binham to **Langham,** where Captain Marryat, writer of sagas of the sea, chose to retire. The church has a tablet to him, a north window by Morris and Burne-Jones, and a Purbeck marble font.

Continue on the B1388 to **Blakeney**. The quay here is one of the beauty spots of Norfolk, popular with artists who come to paint the view across the salt marshes. The village is well preserved and has many flint-built cottages. The church has a slender beacon turret, a hammerbeam roof and interesting misericords. Further along the A149 is **Cley.** Once over the bridge (the river Glaven) turn right, away from the town, to the church at Newgate. Originally cruciform in design (the transepts are now in ruins) it has a fine south porch. One of the bosses over the door shows a woman chasing a fox. Inside there are many carved figures, a lovely font with the Seven Sacraments, and several brasses.

Return to the A149 and follow it into Cley, a charming town, once a port greater than King's Lynn, but now, because of silting, over a mile from the sea. A road leads off left over the marshes towards **Blakeney Point,** a shingle bank famous for its bird life and now a sanctuary under the National Trust. Continue through **Salthouse,** another former port and birthplace of Admiral Sir Christopher Myngs, and follow the coast road away from the flats to the cliffs that lay to the east of **Weybourne.** The Angles are thought to have made their first landing in England at Weybourne, and the Danes followed them centuries later. This attractive village, sheltered by the surrounding hills, has a pretty church and the ruins of an Augustinian priory. At the side of these a road leads to the beach where there is good fishing. From opposite the church a road leads across Kelling Heath to Holt. The B1149 leads from Holt back to Norwich.

ROUTE 4

KING'S LYNN — Castle Rising — Sandringham — Hunstanton — Brancaster — Hillington — KING'S LYNN (about 44 miles).

Leave **King's Lynn** (see page 32) by the A149 signposted to Hunstanton and continue to **Castle Rising,** once a grand seaport returning two members to Parliament, but now only a small village with a ruined castle. The castle (plate 13) (open to the public) was built in 1150 and used by Edward III to hold his mother Queen Isabella, after her implication in the death of her husband, Edward II. It changed hands several times after this, and ultimately was bought by the Howard family who still own it. The massive Norman keep is one of the largest in England and is reached by a bridge over the inner moat. The parish church is mainly Norman with a carved Norman font. Opposite is Bede House, a hospital for widows and spinsters founded by the Howards in 1614. The ladies still wear red cloaks and Jacobean hats when attending church on Sundays. The village green has a market cross.

Continue along the A149, cross the **Babingley** River (notice the ruined church in the marsh on the left, founded by St. Felix in the 7th century) and fork right on to the B1439. This road runs through the **Sandringham** estate to West Newton where you turn left on to the B1440 up to the gates of Sandringham Park. The park is open on Wednesdays and Thursdays in the summer when the Court is absent. The church contains many memorials to the Royal Family.

Rejoin the A149 at Dersingham and continue north through **Snettisham,** where carr-stone, the local sandstone, is quarried, to **Heacham.** This village was the home of John Rolfe who went to Virginia in the early 17th century and returned to Heacham with his Indian bride Pocahontas. There is a memorial to the princess in the church. A road leads from the village to the beach, which is a popular holiday centre.

Drive on between lavender fields to **Hunstanton**, an old fishing port and a rapidly growing holiday centre with swimming pool, boating lake, garden of rest, etc. The road passes New Hunstanton first and then the old town, and swings east away from the cliffs to the salt flat of the north Norfolk coast. Return can be made to Lynn either back along the A149 or by following the coast road through the little lost ports of Holme, Thornham and Titchwell to Brancaster and thence inland through Docking and Hillington to Lynn. **Brancaster** was a Roman fort, one of a number built to protect the country from the invasions of Germanic tribes. It was garrisoned by Dalmatian cavalry, an interesting comment on the cosmopolitan nature of the Roman army.

Take the B1153 on the right and drive across open downland through Docking (where turn right along the A1067 and then left on to the B1153) and on towards Hillington. **Flitcham** village has an attractive sign depicting the arrival of St. Felix from Burgundy. Several of these signs, each portraying a local legend, were erected in the villages around

Sandringham by George V. At **Hillington**—another carr-stone village, with fine monuments in the church—the A148 leads back to Lynn.

ROUTE 5.

THETFORD — East Wretham — Watton — Swaffham — Castle Acre — Oxborough — Grimes Graves — Brandon — THETFORD (about 61 miles).

From **Thetford** (see page 39) take the A11 north for about two miles then fork left for **East Wretham,** site of a battle in 1010 between the English and the Danes. This is the heart of the **Breckland**, the stretch of sandy heathland that was the home of the great bustard, a goose-sized bird which was exterminated in the last century. The bleak meres are now frequented by migrating wildfowl and the stone-curlew. The Breckland was also a battle training ground and many of the isolated cottages have been left in ruins by military manoeuvres.

Follow the road to Great Hockham where turn left for Watton, joining the B1111 for the last three miles. About a mile north of the junction with B1077 to Attleborough you pass **Wayland Wood** on the right. This is the supposed scene of the story of the 'Babes in the Wood'. **Watton** is a plain market town that suffered a widespread fire in 1673. The clock-tower in the centre of the town was built to hold a fire bell to prevent the tragedy recurring. On the tower is a weather-vane with a hare (locally called a 'wat') and a tun barrel. The church has an amusing 17th century collecting box in the shape of an old man.

Leave Watton, going west by the Swaffham road, and shortly turn right on the B1077. Continue another mile and turn left to **Great Cressingham,** worthy of attention because of its beautiful 15th century manor, one of Norfolk's finest brick buildings. Through this village the road soon joins the A1065. Turn right on to it and drive to Swaffham.

Swaffham is a pleasant town and its Perpendicular church has a fine double hammerbeam roof covered with angels. The domed market cross is topped by Ceres, goddess of the harvest. The town sign and carvings in the church represent the Pedlar of Swaffham, a figure in local legends. The story goes that one day in London he was told to return to Swaffham to find buried treasure. He did so, became rich, and endowed Swaffham church. Due north, just off the A1065, is **Castle Acre.** The Norman baron, William de Warrenne, built the castle here, and the north gate still stands in Bailey Street. Little else of the building remains, but the ruins of Castle Acre Priory (plate 11), a Department of the Environment property, are much more impressive. This was founded by the same de Warrenne for Cluniac monks. The west front of the priory church is a beautiful example of Norman work with intricate dog-tooth decoration around the centre doorway.

Return to Swaffham and near the church take the minor right turn to the delightful sounding village of **Cockley Cley.** The road goes across heath and plantation, through the village and on to **Oxborough.** Over the crossroads you come to Oxburgh Hall, a National Trust property, built in 1482 (plate 16). A moated, castellated house with a superb brick gate-tower, it has a priest's hole (the owners were Roman Catholics) and when mass was about to be said, washing was hung out as a signal to worshippers. The road continues on to Stoke Ferry on the A134. Turn left here and drive back towards Thetford.

Continue along this road for seven miles until you reach the forestry plantations around **Mundford.** Two miles on, the B1108 crosses at Lynford. Turn right for **Grimes Graves** and after half a mile a track leads off to the left to this famous prehistoric site. Excavations here uncovered elaborate flint quarries made by Stone Age man searching for good flints for weapons and tools. There are nearly 300 shallow pits from which have been taken many implements and bones. The B1108 continues on to join the A1065 which leads to **Brandon,** actually in Suffolk, which was a flint knapping centre. The craft is continued behind the Flint Knappers Arms, supplying museums with flints for their ancient fire arms. From the town centre the B1107 leads back through more of Thetford Chase forest to Thetford.

ROUTE 6

NORWICH — Caistor St. Edmund — Harleston — Scole — Diss — South Lopham — Attleborough — Wymondham — Swardeston — NORWICH (about 65 miles).

Leave **Norwich** by the A146 to Lowestoft. On the outskirts of the town the road crosses the River Yare and shortly after, in Trowse Newton, take the right hand turn to **Caistor St. Edmund.** A mile further on, the electricity pylons run close to the road and beneath them is the site of a 'Woodhenge',

1. Elm Hill, Norwich

Hallam Ashley

2. Bonner's Cottages at East Dereham

3. The Market Cross, Wymondham

4. (right) The Fishermen's Hospital at Great Yarmouth

5. *Norfolk reed thatching at Horning*

6. *Sailing on the Waveney*

7. *(right). The tower mill at Burnham Overy.*

J. W. Whitela

8. Norwich Castle now houses an excellent museum. Hallam Ashley

9. Keeping up an old custom, the Bishop of Norwich visits his abbey of St. Benet's-at-Hulme, near Horning.

R. D. Barrett-Lennard

Hallam Ashley

10. The East window of St. Peter Mancroft, Norwich, has 15th century glass illustrating Bible stories.

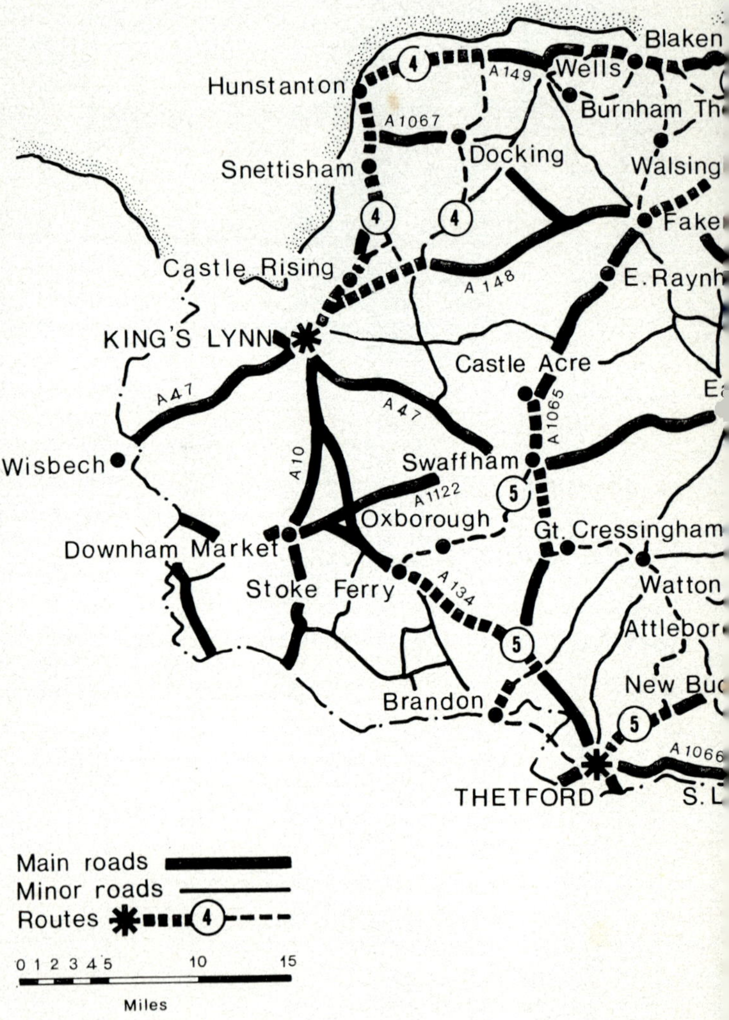

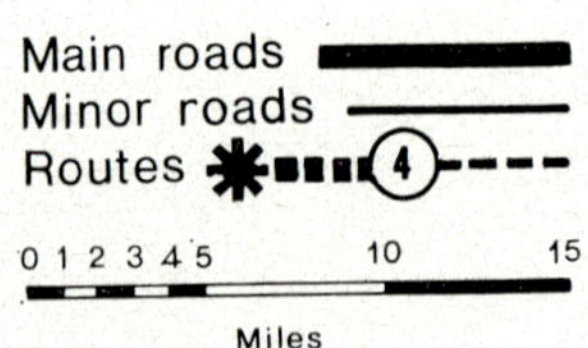
Hunstanton
Wells
Burnham
A 149
A 1067
Docking
Snettisham
Walsing
Castle Rising
A 148
E. Raynh
KING'S LYNN
Castle Acre
A 47
A 47
A 1065
A 10
Wisbech
Swaffham
A 1122
Oxborough
Gt. Cressingham
Downham Market
Stoke Ferry
A 134
Watton
Attlebor
New Bu
Brandon
A 1066
THETFORD
Main roads
Minor roads
Routes
4
5
0 1 2 3 4 5 10 15
Miles

Weybourne
Cley
Sheringham
Cromer
A 148
HOLT
Felbrigg
Paston
2
N. Walsham
Aylsham
2
A 1151
A 149
A 140
Potter Heigham
A 1067
Wroxham
1
1
ereham
2
S. Walsham
Caister
47
A 1064
Acle
NORWICH
1
Gt. YARMOUTH
A 47
6
Caistor St. Edmund
Wymondham
A 146
A 12
A 11
A 143
Long Stratton
A 140
Lowestoft
6
am
Bungay
Beccles
ham
St. Mary
A 143
6
Harleston
Diss
m
Scole

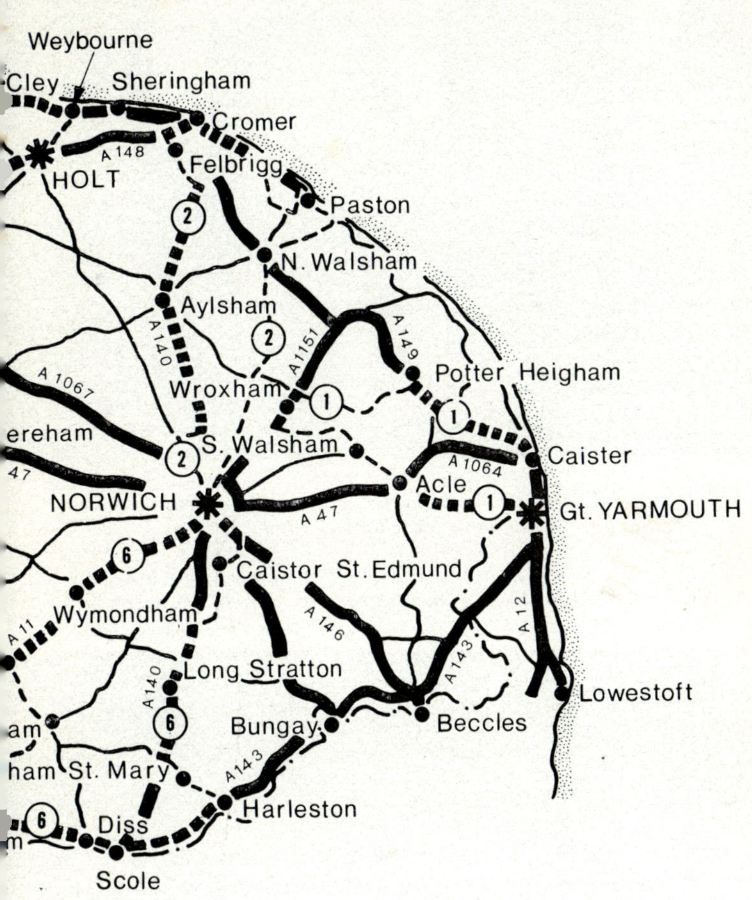

NORFOLK

J. W. Whitelaw

11. *Castle Acre Priory was founded by the Norman baron, William de Warrenne, for Cluniac monks.*

12. *The late Saxon cathedral at North Elmham was constructed about 1000 A.D. This view shows the interior of the nave from the east.*

Dept. of Environment

Hallam Ashley

13. The stairway entrance to the keep at Castle Rising. Edward III had his mother imprisoned here.

Leon Metcalfe

14. *Blickling Hall is reputedly haunted by Anne Boleyn, whose home it once was.*

15. *The Norfolk Wildlife Park at Great Witchingham was where the first otters were born in captivity in Britain for 84 years.*

Hallam Ashley

Doris Nicholson

16. Oxburgh Hall is a fine fifteenth century house, now owned by the National Trust.

17. East Barsham Manor, where Henry VIII once slept, is near Walsingham.

J. W. Whitelaw

18. A view of the Broads near Horsey Mere.

19. These fine barley-sugar columns flank the entrance to a courtyard at King's Lynn.

20. The Customs House, King's Lynn, was built in 1683.

a prehistoric circle of oak posts, now defined only by two enclosing ditches.

Caistor is the site of the Roman town of Venta Icenorum and the chief town of the Celtic Iceni of whom Boadicea was queen. Over the crossroads in the village the road passes, on the right, the parish church which stands in the walled enclosure of the Roman town. The church has the earliest dated example of an 'East Anglian' font—decorated with lions, emblems of the Trinity and the Passion. Follow the same road to the start of Stoke Holy Cross where turn right, cross the River Tas by a mill, turn left and wind round to meet the A140. Turn left and motor south towards Scole. This was the Roman road from Caistor St. Edmund to Colchester. It passes through **Long Stratton,** worth stopping at to see St. Mary's church (the one with the round tower) which has an old sexton's wheel used for determining fast days. Three miles further on turn left to Harleston, through the delightful villages of **Pulham Market** and **Pulham St. Mary.** From **Harleston,** a pretty little village of Georgian houses, follow the A143 along the valley to **Scole**, where the Scole Inn stands. This was once the best known inn on the coach road from Ipswich to Norwich and had an elaborate gallows sign that bridged the road and was the wonder of the district.

From Scole the A1066 runs west to **Diss**, a bright little town with pleasant shops and many old buildings. The grand Decorated church, much restored, has two 15th century chapels off the chancel. Follow the A1066 to **South Lopham** and turn right along the B1113 to the parish church, whose five-stage tower is one of the best Norman church towers in the county. Note the Norman west doorway and the intricate poppy-heads. B1113 takes you to **Kenninghall.** Here there was once a manor where Queen Mary waited after Edward VI's death and during the plot to keep her from the throne.

A road from here leads north to **Snetterton,** a centre for motor racing; but a more pleasant drive follows the B1113 through **Banham,** a cider-making village to **New Buckenham,** a large village with an old market cross and a whipping post. Return from the village to the crossroads and take the B1077 right through **Old Buckenham** (a road on the right leads to the ruins of a Norman keep) to **Attleborough.** The church here has a fine 16th century screen, second only to Ranworth in the whole county. Take the A11 to **Wymondham** (see page 39) and from here either straight back to Norwich or at **Cringleford** make a short diversion by turning right just after the church and following signs to **Swardeston.** Nurse Edith

Cavell was born at the vicarage and the church proudly displays the wooden cross from her first grave in Flanders. (She is now buried by Norwich Cathedral.) The B1113 leads on to Norwich.

MAIN PLACES OF INTEREST

CROMER Route 2

E.C. Wednesday, Population 5,550

One of Jane Austen's characters called Cromer 'the best of all sea-bathing places', and the town was a popular resort throughout the 19th century. Its sandy beaches and dry bracing weather still attract holiday visitors. A massive sea wall has halted the erosion of Cromer's cliffs. The town centre clusters around the **church.** The tower is over 160 feet and the tallest of any Norfolk parish church. The closeness of the town cottages accentuates this upward thrust. Unfortunately the old chancel was demolished with gunpowder in the 17th century to save money on its upkeep. It has been restored and the present chancel is 19th century. In the streets and alleys leading from the church there are some pleasant shops.

DOWNHAM MARKET

M.D. Friday, E.C. Wednesday, Population 3,340

The draining of the fens in the extreme west of Norfolk has since the 17th century brought into production the rich arable area around Downham, which serves as its market town. Charles I, disguised as a clergyman, came here after the battle of Naseby. He was on his way north to Scotland. Nelson was educated at the school here, now **Nelson House** in Bridge Street, so was George Manby, inventor of the rocket lifesaving apparatus. The 15th century **church** has a fine angel roof, now attractively re-coloured, and the remains of a medieval preaching cross.

EAST DEREHAM

M.D. Friday, E.C. Wednesday, Population 8,390

The town sign spanning the main street recalls the legend of St. Withburga who founded a nunnery here in 645 A.D. At one time the nunnery was short of food and, in answer to Withburga's prayers, two does appeared each day to provide milk. A local huntsman set his dogs upon the deer but in the chase he fell from his horse and was killed. The shrine and tomb of St. Withburga is close to **St. Nicholas' church,** which has a separate bell tower. Also nearby are the attractive thatched **Bonner's Cottages,** in which there is a museum of local history (plate 2).

GREAT YARMOUTH Route 1

M.D. Wednesday and Saturday, E.C. Thursday, Population 50,760

Even if you dislike large busy seaside resorts there is much worth seeing in Yarmouth. The centre of the town is the **market place** with stalls selling shellfish, chips and hot peas. Start your tour here, and make for King Street on the south side. To your right, linking King Street and the Quay are the famous **Rows,** originally 145 narrow passages, some only three feet wide, called by Dickens 'the Norfolk gridiron'. Many rows have been blocked up, and some destroyed in the bombing of the 1939-45 war.

Yarmouth Way leads to Tolhouse Street and the old **Tolhouse,** a 13th century building with an outside staircase. It was used at one time as a prison. Completely gutted during the war, it has now been restored. Walk through to **No. 4 South Quay,** which is the museum of art and local history. The building was originally Elizabethan and in the drawing room on the first floor the Parliamentary leaders are supposed to have decided the fate of Charles I. Note the fine plaster ceiling. Continue down South Quay with the herring steamers on your right and at Row 117 is the **Old Merchant's House,** a Department of the Environment property, open daily.

Return through the Rows to King Street and the Market Place. To the north lies Church Plain, on the right of which is the **Fishermen's Hospital** (plate 4), a delightful building, built in 1702 and consisting of tiny almshouses around a cobbled cloister. The statue in the middle is Charity and on the roof cupola is St. Peter, patron-saint of fishermen.

Between the Hospital and the Vicarage is half-timbered **Sewell House** where Anna Sewell, authoress of *Black Beauty*, lived. The Vicarage is another fine 18th century building. From here walk to **St. Nicholas Church**, in area the largest parish church in England. It was gutted by fire in 1942 but has since been completely restored. The nave dates from the 12th century, and the aisles, the widest in England, were added in the 13th century. St. Nicholas Road leads from Church

Plain to the beach and to Yarmouth's famous holiday attractions—two piers, swimming baths, Marina, pleasure gardens, boating lakes, recreation parks—and the original **Nelson Column,** erected in 1817.

KING'S LYNN Route 4

M.D. Tuesday, E.C. Wednesday, Population 30,650

Lynn is perhaps one of the most perfect towns in England —a model of proportion and planning when these virtues were practised voluntarily. The attractive streets and buildings make it more akin to a Flemish than an English town. King John made Lynn a free borough in 1204 (just before he lost his crown in the Wash). It was a busy sea port and its trade increased tremendously as the country inland was opened up by canals. The railway took away some of this trade but as a port it still serves much of the East Midlands. Start a tour of Lynn from **Saturday Market Place,** at the end of St. James's Street, off London Road. The market place has a car park. **St. Margaret's Church** is the first building to visit. Built by the Norman Bishop Losinga, who also built Norwich Cathedral, it is noted for its two 14th century Flemish brasses—the largest in the country. One illustrates a vintage, the other a peacock feast in honour of Edward III. Fanny Burney's father was organist here. On the opposite side of Saturday Market Place is the 15th century **Guildhall,** faced with flint and stone in black and white check.

Now follow Queen Street past **Thoresby's College** for priests to the famous **Customs House** (plate 20), built in 1683, with a statue of Charles II over the door. Then continue along into King Street past **St. George's Guildhall,** centre for the annual festival, to **Tuesday Market Place,** the most prosperous-looking part of Lynn. Around the square are the Corn Exchange and the old houses of the wealthy merchants. The Mart, held here on February 14th for over 800 years, used to be the earliest fair of the year in England. The square was also the place for public hangings and witch burnings. From the north-east of the square you reach **St. Nicholas's Chapel,** a 15th century church with a long angel roof and a beautiful south porch. Look for the floor slab to Robinson Crusoe (not Defoe's fictitious hero—only a namesake). Return down Chapel Street and Broad Street, turn right, and visit the **Greenland Fishery Building,** a half-timbered house built in 1605, now completely restored after being damaged during the Second World War.

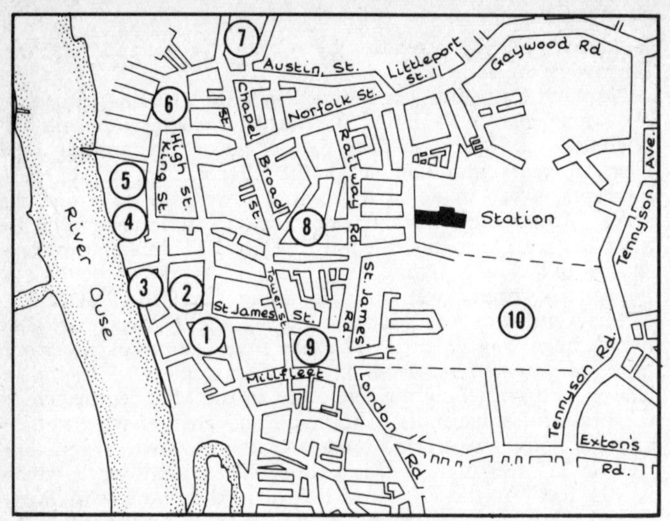

1 St. Margaret's Church
2 Guildhall
3 Thoresby's College
4 Customs House
5 St. George's Guildhall
6 Tuesday's Market Place
7 St. Nicholas's Chapel
8 Greenland Fishery Building
9 Greyfriar Tower
10 Red Mount Chapel

Cross Blackfriars into Tower Street, which brings you to the **Greyfriar Tower** in St. James's. This slender hexagonal shaft is all that is left of a 13th Century friary, and of the dozen or more religious houses in Lynn which were suppressed by Henry VIII. St. James's Street takes you back to Saturday Market Place. Before leaving Lynn visit the Walks on the east of London Road. The **Red Mount Chapel** overlooks this public park. The plain exterior belies the exquisite chapel inside, a perfect 15th century confection.

NORWICH — Routes 2 and 6

M.D. Wednesday and Saturday, E.C. Thursday, Population 118,800.

Start your tour of the city at the Cathedral. There are two gates from Tombland to the Cathedral Precinct. Take the northern one (opposite the Sampson and Hercules House), called the **Erpingham Gate,** built by Sir Thomas Erpingham in 1420. (Sir Thomas appears in Shakespeare's *Henry V.*) The west front of the Cathedral faces you and the **King Edward IV**

Grammar School attended by Coke, Nelson and George Borrow is on your left.

Norwich Cathedral was founded in 1096 by Bishop Losinga, the same man who built St. Margaret's at Lynn and St. Nicholas's at Yarmouth. The first phase of the building took over 50 years and completed the chancel, apsidal chapels, transepts, lower stages of the central tower, the nave and the aisles. Most of this work remains today, making Norwich the most perfect Norman cathedral in England. Note the massive square pillars and semi-circular arches. At the same time a Benedictine priory was built adjoining the Cathedral.

The Cathedral was added to during the 13th century and fire damage was repaired. The fire tinged some of the stone pink, as you can see from the south-east piers of the nave. The second great building phase was in the 15th century when the beautiful stone roofs in the nave and chancel were put up and the spire was erected on top of the Norman tower. The spire is 315 feet high, and is second only to Salisbury's which is 404 feet. At the end of the nave is the choir with finely carved 15th century stalls and fascinating misericords. The Norman work of the chancel has been overlaid with Decorated and Perpendicular work. It has a semi-circular apse at the east and in the apse stands the Bishop's throne. This uncomfortable seat is the only surviving example of its type in Northern Europe. Research suggests that the arms of the throne are much older than the Cathedral, probably 8th century. In front of the altar rails is a blue slab that marks the burial place of Losinga, founder of the Cathedral. The chancel is surrounded by an ambulatory, or aisle, off which are a number of chapels. On the north side is the Jesus Chapel where relics were displayed to pilgrims from the balcony. Note the 14th century wall paintings. Following the ambulatory round behind the apse you come to St. Saviour's Chapel, built in 1931 as a war memorial. It contains several wonderful medieval paintings. Next is the Norman Chapel of St. Luke, now used as the Parish Church of St. Mary-in-the-Marsh, a church which once stood on the south side of the Cathedral Close. The reredos or altar piece and other painted panels form, with the St. Saviour paintings, the finest group of medieval paintings in England. Last is the Bauchin Chapel with a vaulted roof. Opposite the entrance, between ambulatory and chancel, is the monument to Bishop Goldwell who was responsible for the spate of building in the 15th century. He is shown wearing a cope instead of the usual Communion chasuble. Puritans destroyed most other monuments in the

Cathedral, including Losinga's, and Goldwell's has a musket ball still lodged in it. Nearby is the tomb of Sir William Boleyn, grandfather of Anne Boleyn.

Continue across the south transept to the south aisle. A door on the left leads to the Cloisters, amongst the largest and certainly the most interesting in England. There are nearly 400 carved and painted bosses on the roof. In the north walk they portray scenes from the life of Christ, the life of the Virgin, and the story of Thomas a Becket. The east walk has stories from the Gospels, the south and west stories from the Book of Revelation. To prevent a stiff neck use the mirror mounted on a trolley to examine the bosses.

By the south-east corner of the Cathedral is Life's Green and the simple cross of Nurse Edith Cavell's grave. Before leaving the Cathedral Close walk south-east to **Pull's Ferry**, picturesque and inoperative, and a favourite subject for painters and photographers. Leave the Close by the southern gate, St. Ethelbert's, which was built in the early 1300s with money the town had to pay the monastery for riot damage.

Back in Tombland cross to Queen Street, with its pleasant shops, and at Bank Plain turn right to the **Castle** (plate 8). The entrance is on the south side of the mound. The present building—now a first-class museum—is only the keep of the original castle. It was built about 1150 by Roger Bigod. The present cardboard appearance is due to a refacing it received in the 1830s. The decoration on the walls follows the original and is unique in its abundance. Special attractions inside are the dioramas of Norfolk wild life, the galleries of Crome and Cotman paintings, and dungeons with prisoners' autographs.

From the castle, pass the Bell Hotel and follow Red Lion Street to Rampant Horse Street. Turn right along the latter past St. Stephen's to the **Assembly House,** the best Georgian building in Norwich. Go into the Foyer, the Music Room and the Banqueting Hall (now a restaurant), each beautifully proportioned and decorated. Cross the street to the **Central Library,** opened in 1962. It has a delightful patio with a fascinating mural.

From here go to the **City Hall,** overlooking the Market Place. The Hall was built in 1938 and is still acclaimed as the finest municipal building of the interwar years. There is much of Swedish influence in the design. On the doors are the emblems of the city's various industries. Below the steps is the Garden of Remembrance designed by Sir Edwin Lutyens.

To the south is **St. Peter Mancroft** (plate 10), the finest church in Norwich. Built on the 'Magna Crofta' (great field) of the castle, 1430-55, it is a monument to the riches of the Norwich merchants. Note particularly the large, heavily decorated tower pierced at the base with a processional arch (the silly spire was added in 1894), the east window of 15th century glass, and the fine hammerbeam roof lit by 35 clerestory windows. Sir Thomas Browne, author of *Religio Medici*, is buried here. There is a statue of him south of the church. Walk through the Market Place to the **Guildhall,** a little flint building dating from 1407. The 16th century council chamber (used regularly until the new City Hall was built) has a carved ceiling and linenfold panelling. Among the exhibits is the sword of Spanish Admiral Winthuysen who surrendered to Nelson at Cape St. Vincent.

From the Guildhall walk up towards St. Giles Street and take Lower Goat Lane on the right. Cross Pottergate and follow the cobbled alley under St. Gregory's Church to Charing Cross. Along on the right is **Strangers' Hall,** entered through an old doorway and an attractive courtyard. This merchant's house is now an interesting museum—a series of fine rooms illustrating the history of domestic furniture. The most interesting rooms are the undercroft, the Hall with its beautiful oriel window, and the Georgian Room, dripping with chandelier.

Past the Strangers' Hall turn right into Maddermarket, named after the vegetable dye, madder, used by the Norwich weavers. To the right is the **Maddermarket Theatre,** a repertory theatre built in the Elizabethan style. Ahead is the 15th century St. John's Church, squeezed between two buildings and with a passage beneath. Return from Maddermarket to St. Andrew Street and continue along to St. Andrew's, a fine Perpendicular church with a monument to the parents of Sir John Suckling. The poet was born at Suckling House near the church. Behind the church is the **Bridewell Museum.** The front of knapped flint is a fine example of a local craft. The building dates back to the 14th century, was the home of the first mayor of Norwich, became a jail, and is now a museum of local industries.

Return to St. Andrew's Street, which ends at **St. Andrew's Hall**. This was the church of the Blackfriars of Norwich and is the most complete friars' church existing in England. It was built 1440-70 and was given to the town at the Dissolution for use as an assembly hall. The present St. Andrew's Hall was the nave, Blackfriars Hall adjoining was the chancel. The latter was leased to Flemish Protestants who came to Norwich in the 16th century. From the north aisle of St. Andrew's you can reach the former cloister and domestic buildings of the priory. From St. Andrew's Hall Plain turn north up St. George's Street, cross the River Wensum, to **St. George's Church** in Colegate, where John Crome is buried. This side of the river is the old industrial district of Norwich. Turn right along Colegate. On the left is the **Octagonal Chapel,** built in 1756 by Thomas Ivory, architect of the Assembly House. Originally Presbyterian, it is now a Unitarian House and was called by John Wesley the most elegant in Europe. A little further on the same side of Colegate a passage leads to the **Old Meeting,** a Congregational church built in 1693. This beautiful red brick building was supposedly built away from the road to make it easier to defend against rioters.

Colegate ends at **Magdalene Street.** Do not miss this fascinating experiment in town decoration. Turn left and

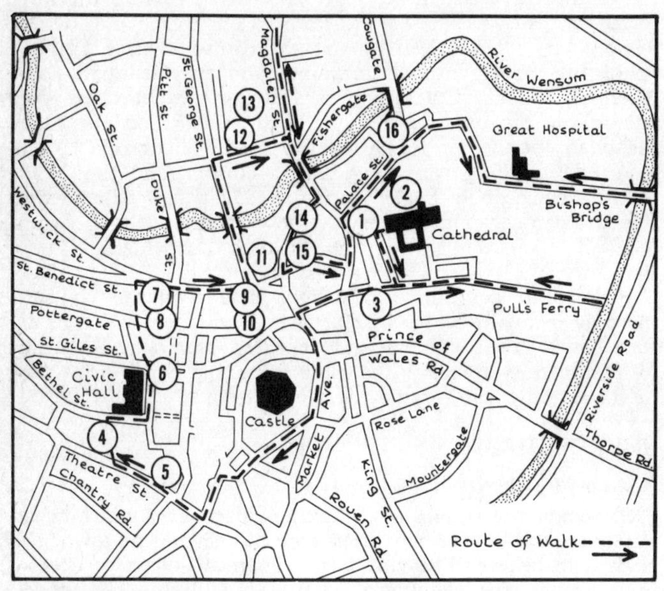

1 Erpingham Gate
2 King Edward Grammar School
3 St. Ethelbert's Gate
4 Central Library
5 St. Peter Mancroft
6 Guildhall
7 Strangers' Hall
8 Maddermarket Theatre
9 St. Andrew's Church
10 Bridewell
11 St. Andrew's Hall
12 Octagonal Chapel
13 Old Meeting
14 Elm Hill
15 St. Peter Hungate
16 Cotman's House

walk along this shopping street, chosen by the Civic Trust to be its first venture in facelifting modern Britain. Note the attractive colouring and lettering on the shop fronts, the 'toy town' bank, and the carefully designed street lighting. So successful was this scheme (begun in 1958) that it has been extended to the Market Place, St. Benedicts and Tombland.

Return along Magdalene Street over the river into Wensum Street. The first right turn is **Elm Hill** (plate 1), a cobbled lane lined with the fine houses of merchants, now pleasant shops. The Strangers' Club, Pettus House and Flint House are perhaps the best. At the bend stands the elm from which Elm Hill takes its name. At the top of Elm Hill is Princes Street. Turn left past **St. Peter Hungate,** rebuilt by the Paston family in 1460 and now a church museum, and walk down towards Tombland where we began.

For the energetic, there is yet another quarter of the town worth a visit. Palace Street, leading off Tombland by the Maid's Head Hotel leads to **St. Martin's-at-Palace Plain,** a delightful corner with church, inn, and the Georgian house where the painter Cotman lived. Leaving the church to your left follow the winding road to Bishopsgate and the **Great Hospital,** founded in 1249 for the aged. The wards of this charming building were originally a church, and the ceiling of the chancel, now Eagle Ward, has 252 panels painted with the Austrian eagle, in memory of the visit of Anne of Bohemia, wife of Richard II. See the hospital chapel, the Tudor Refectory, the cloisters and the swan pit.

Bishopsgate continues to **Bishops Bridge** on the Wensum, the only medieval bridge in Norwich. It was across this bridge that Kett's rebels entered and captured Norwich. Returning to Tombland you follow the same route that Kett's army took in its running battle with the Royal troops.

SHERINGHAM

E.C. Wednesday, Population 5,040.

Sheringham was once a tiny fishing village. Looking at the late Victorian and Edwardian brick core of the present town, this is hard to believe. The village has 'boomed' into a prosperous resort—not with jangling funfairs—but with a featureless dedication to the manufacture of sunny, sandy holidays. Besides the usual resort attractions, the town has some pretty spots—like Pretty Corner and Sheringham Park (landscaped by Repton) and is well placed for excursions along the Norfolk coast and south into the depths of the country.

THETFORD

Route 5

M.D. Wednesday and Saturday, E.C. Wednesday, Population 11,640.

Domesday Book lists the five greatest towns in England as London, York, Norwich, Winchester and Thetford. In the 14th century Thetford had several monasteries and twenty churches. Today this shrunken little town, surrounded by some of the wildest country in southern England, has embarked on a new role as an overspill for Greater London. Thetford's eerie position between the Siberian woods of the Forestry Commission and the rough battle training grounds of the Breckland echoes its turbulent past. Paleolithic, Neolithic and Roman remains have all been found here, and Sweyn the Norseman burnt the town in 1004.

Present-day visitors should visit **Castle Hill**; the **priory** remains near the railway station; **St. Mary's church** on the Suffolk side of the Little Ouse; and **Tom Paine's statue.** Paine was born here in 1737. Embittered by life and his calling as a stay-maker, he went to America, becoming an ardent revolutionary. He fired the imagination of the colonists when he wrote *The Rights of Man* and is remembered as 'the Father of the American Revolution'. The modern statue caused much controversy, Paine being considered, quite rightly, a traitor by some Thetford citizens. At one time he subscribed money to Napoleon's projected invasion of Britain.

WYMONDHAM

Route 6

M.D. Friday, E.C. Wednesday, Population 7,810.

Called 'Windham', this was the home of Robert Kett, the rebel who raised the peasants of Norfolk to arms in 1549. The **Market Cross** of Kett's day was replaced by the present one in 1618 (plate 3), and this was restored in the last century.

Wymondham **church** has two towers and a turbulent history. It was originally the church of the Benedictine abbey but conflicts between monks and townsfolk led to it being partitioned, the chancel being reserved for the monks and the nave for the town. The octagonal east tower went to the abbey so the town built the west tower (never completed). After the Dissolution by Henry VIII the chancel was destroyed, so the present church is only the nave of the original Norman structure. The aisles were built in the 15th and 16th centuries. By the church is St. Thomas a Becket's well, a former place of pilgrimage.

INDEX TO PLACES

Printed by C. I. Thomas & Sons (Haverfordwest) Ltd., Press Buildings, Merlin's Bridge, Haverfordwest, Pembrokeshire.